AMAZONIAN TRIBES: A WORLD OF DIFFERENCE

Northwater

CONSTANTINE ISSIGHOS

Copyright 2012 © Constantine Issighos. Published in Canada. Printed in U.S.A. No part of this book may be reproduced or transmitted in any form or by any means, electronic or mechanical, including photocopying, recording, and/or by any information storage and retrieval system except by a reviewer who may quote brief passages in a review to be printed in a magazine, newspaper, or on the web without written permission in writing from the author/publisher. For information, please contact www.awaqkunabooks.com

NorthWater is an imprint of Awaqkuna Books Inc.

Vol. 11 of THE AMAZON EXPLORATION SERIES:

AMAZONIAN TRIBES:
A WORLD OF DIFFERENCE

Library and Archives Canada

ISBN 978-0-9878601-0-1

Library and Archives Canada Cataloguing in Publication

ATTENTION CHILDRENS ASSOCIATIONS, BOOK STORES, PUBLIC OR PRIVATE LIBRARIES: quantity discounts are available on bulk purchases of this book series.

THE AMAZON EXPLORATION SERIES

Children's Books
by
Constantine Issighos

1	Upper Amazon Voyage by River Boat
2	The People of the River
3	The Children of the River
4	Amazon's Nature of Things
5	Echoes of Nature: a Beautiful Wild Habitat
6	The Amazon Rainforest
7	Amazonian Sisterhood
8	Amazon River Wolves
9	Amazonian Landscapes and Sunsets
10	Amazonian Canopy: the Roof of the World's Rainforest
11	Amazonian Tribes: a World of Difference
12	Birds, Flowers and Butterflies of the Amazon
13	The Great Wonders of the Amazon
14	The Jaguar People
15	The Fresh Water Giants
16	The Call of the Shaman
17	Indigenous Families: Life in Harmony with Nature
18	Amazon in Peril
19	Giant Tarantulas and Centipedes
20	The Amazon Ethno-Botanical Garden
21	The Real Amazon Tribal Warriors

The Amazon is a vast rainforest. Its ecosystem is without parallel. Scientists are continually making new discoveries and raising intriguing questions in a quest for future preservation strategies. When it comes to inspiring wonder, the Amazon rainforest has no rival.

Occupying 5.5 million square kilometres of the most species-rich forest anywhere, it is breathtaking in its biodiversity, from the towering canopies to millions of different living species. Covering 7 million square kilometres and spread over 9 nations, it is the world's largest reserve of fresh water. Its vast green stretches along its hundreds of muddy tributaries, appearing primitive and timeless. Yet its remoteness and sheer size makes the Amazon self-protective of its secrets—some of which are being revealed slowly as new plant, animal life and indigenous tribe discoveries are made.

Covering almost a third of the Peruvian territory, the Upper Amazon is densely vegetated and criss-crossed by navigable rivers and tributaries; the interior of the Department of Loreto is rarely visited and sparsely populated. Indeed, so-called uncontacted indigenous tribes still inhabit some of its forests.

Overall, the Amazon indigenous tribes have a very long history of human settlement. Presently, there are about half a million tribesmen who are divided among an estimated 500 tribes, including about 75 uncontacted tribes still living in voluntary isolation. There are still about 220 indigenous groups, sharing 175 different dialects and each with their own social structure and cultural heritage. Some of these spoken dialects share common terms and meanings, and if one narrows the scope to linguistic families one will find 30 distinct languages. This shows that the cultural diversity in the region is as rich as the flora and fauna.

Since the Amazon region is made up of different biological environments, the indigenous people have adapted their culture to the various ecosystems. The majority of the tribes live in the tropical rainforest, while others live in grasslands and pampas—plains—or in semi-desert areas. Because of the variety of ecosystems in which they live, their material culture is modified to allow them to adapt and survive. Depending on the region in which they live, and the particular Amazon tribe to which they belong, they have various degrees of contact with and influence from the outside world. This would be expected, as the Amazon rainforest itself is divided among 9 different countries—Bolivia, Brazil, Colombia, Ecuador, French Guyana, Guyana, Peru, Suriname and Venezuela.

These indigenous people became attuned to the ecological realities of the rainforest through 5,000 years of accumulated knowledge, with a solid understanding of how to manage their ecosystem to meet the requirements of their subsistence. They saw the importance of a balanced ecology through the preservation of natural forests, open fields and the management of forest sections dominated by animal life of great use to the tribe. Alongside this balanced dialectical approach to nature, the tribal spiritual activities also accommodated the tribe's emotional needs. These spiritual ceremonies were conducted by the tribe's shaman.

The practice of shamanism is an important aspect of understanding the indigenous world of differences. I hope that the reader will be inspired to think about the importance of shamanic ideology as related to the traditional hunter-gatherer Amazonian societies.

It is reasonable to assume that the origins of the shamanic belief system date back farther than western state religion. Archaeological evidence demonstrates that the shamanic belief system has been an element of the Amazonian human experience for at least 5 millennia. Magical hallucinogens have also been intimately connected with prehistoric communities.

Amazonian shamans are very powerful men who are prominent figures in their tribes. They are distinguished from other tribal men because they are the sole masters of the ecstatic ceremonial experience. Mastering such ceremonial processes enables shamans to transcend into the spiritual world through their songs and chants, which are essential criteria of their acquired power. It is believed that a shaman is able to leave his body to explore the extra-human domain. The shaman's pursuit of power is a never-ending journey, and among those established shamans some are more powerful than others.

The shamanic belief system is also shared and followed by indigenous people who believe in the realm of the spirits as it relates to the immediate ecosystem of the animal world. Many of the indigenous people's myths, legends and folklore relate to and connect with the mystical strength of a chosen animal such as the eagle, condor, boa or jaguar. Such cultural belief systems are shared by the *Ashanikas,* the *Pirahas* and *the Ye'kuana* tribes, all living in the Amazon region but thousands miles apart.

Proud of their culture, the *Ashanikas* are driven by a strong sense of freedom; they stood up to invaders, including the Inca Empire. They possess an astonishing capacity to reconcile traditional customs and values with western ideas and practices concerning socio-environmental sustainability. The term *"Ashanikas"* signifies good spirits who live "above" (*hemoki*).

The *Ashanikas* constitute the main components of the sub-Andean *Aruak* group. Despite the existence of dialect differences among *Ashanikas* groups, the tribe, as a whole, reveals substantial cultural and linguistic homogeneity.

Throughout their history, the *Ashanikas* have had continuous peaceful trade relations with other tribes and non-Indians. These trade contacts have shaped the different group characteristics within the *Ashanikas* tribe. Products, such as animals, skins, feathers, wood, cotton and medicinal plants were traded for cloth, but especially metal objects—silver, gold and machetes—and these items were distributed through the kinship networks of the *Ashanikas* tribe.

We can observe in the *Ashanikas* tribe the cultural characteristics that make up their shamanistic cosmological belief system of a universe divided into various levels—the invisible world behind the visible world—and the role of the shaman as the mediator between the two worlds. In this extreme dualistic conception of the universe, there is a clear and defined boundary between Good and Evil.

The vertically arranged *Ashanikas* spiritual world is comprised of an indeterminate number of superimposed levels: Hell *(Sarikaveni)*, the First Subterranean Level *(Kivinti)*, the Terrestrial World *(Kamaveni)*, the World of Clouds *(Menkori)*, and a set of Celestial Levels *(Kenoki)*. All these are situated between the Earth and the Heavens. Thus, the visible world in which we live is not inhabited solely by human beings, animals and plants; we are constantly threatened by the struggles between Good and Evil.

In contrast to other indigenous tribes in the interior of the Upper Amazon, the *Ashanikas* who live in the lower region of the Amazon have always used cloth. The traditional garment *(Kushma)* is distinctive. The term *Kushma* is used to refer to the garment, the loom and the cloth.

The *Ashanikas* appear to have always had dugout canoes *(Pitotsi)*, homes *(Pakotsi)*, and gardens *(Owatsi)* with several varieties of fruits, vegetables and medicinal plants. Due to the seasonal flooding levels, their homes are not built directly on the ground; they are built on stilts. The homes of the *Ashanikas* follow their traditional structure. They are built without walls or interior divisions. Non-Indian inhabitants, who live in the *Ashanikas* territory, also live in raised homes, but with walls and interior divisions.

The *Pirahas* tribe lives in a pure "state of nature." They depend for their daily subsistence on what nature can provide for them. They are excellent hunters, fishermen and gatherers of fruits and medicinal plants. Their hunting style resembles that of their revered jaguar, sudden and deadly. Their approach to living encompasses only the "here and now." They have not living historical or cultural accounts of past generations. They only go as far back as their present living relatives. They have no art to speak of and their spiritual legends are extremely limited. They do not have regular eating or sleeping habits. They tend to sleep for 15 minutes to 2 hours maximum at various times of the day or night. Their language does not contain specific words for exact numbers, and they have no concept of numeracy.

The *Ye'kuana* tribe consists of about 5,000 people divided among three communities located along the riverbanks of the *Auaris* and *Uraricoera* rivers in the northern Brazilian state of *Rorama*. The *Ye'kuana* maintain their food traditions and their ways of producing this food. They are mainly agriculturalists with large and bountiful gardens. They are also hunters, fishermen and gatherers and they keep small domestic animals, especially birds. They are highly skilled craftsmen of dugout canoes. They burn the center out of a huge tree to construct a dugout canoe for themselves and for other tribes in the area.

The *Ye'kuana* are known for maintaining a very traditional tribal life-style and for having an advanced culture. They are among the most artistic indigenous of the Amazon rainforest. This is reflected in their sculptures and in the intricate patterned designs of their baskets. Both men and women of the *Ye'kuana* tribe weave baskets using traditional design belonging to one or the other gender. Young eligible men must weave flat or tray baskets with the "family crest" and present them to the woman they want to marry. Before marriage, the couple must demonstrate their artistic talents by producing various baskets that the woman will use in running her household.

Women weave traditional round baskets with beautiful geometric designs. These baskets are used as containers in the home. Vase or bell-shaped baskets are also made by the women of the tribe. The shape of the basket follows the general shape of a woman's body—the baskets are small, curved and made to fit snugly onto the woman's back.

Baskets are not just for utility. They have an aesthetic and cultural meaning. Straight twill-weaved baskets are male, while curved, wicker-weaved baskets are female. Each stage of a person's lifecycle is marked by a reciprocal exchange of baskets between genders.

Indigenous homes that are located near the riverbanks are built on stilts and are covered with straw. Each family builds its own shelter with the help of close family members. Other tribes, however, have a more communal social structure for shelters.

Traditional village structures which are designed for indigenous communal living can be found in cleared forest areas. Cleared land in the circular shape in the middle of the forest indicates the presence of an indigenous habitat. Such a clearing is divided in designated zones which are arranged in concentric circles.

The most prominent is the communal house, which is located in the center of the clearing. It has a rounded base and a cone-shaped roof. It has a living capacity for about 60 to 80 people. Its internal space is divided into circular sections where communal meals are cooked and where festivals are held. At night it becomes the sleeping quarters for young single men. Additional circular walled compartments provide shelters for extended families.

Surrounding the communal house there is a designated space for the village women to use for ceremonies and meetings. Following the circular pattern of the village there are small work-structures, one per family. These rectangular shaped structures have a simple two sloped roof—supported by posts—and no walls. Men use the work-house to make or fix their hunting and fishing gear, and to work on their crafts. Women use the work-house to scrape manioc, cook and sew and scrape manioc. The men are excellent canoe-makers and navigators. Their dugout canoes are used to commute to various health-posts and schools along the riverbanks in the indigenous areas.

Each work-house has its own vegetable garden where women cultivate tobacco, cotton, medicinal plants and sugarcane. The far side of the gardens marks the end of the village land. This concentric pattern is repeated at other tribal forest clearings where a visitor can see similar communal living arrangements.

The Amazon Exploration Series *Constantine Issighos*

Amazonian Tribes: A World of Difference 13

The Amazon Exploration Series   *Constantine Issighos*

The Amazon Exploration Series   *Constantine Issighos*

Amazonian Tribes: A World of Difference   *19*

The Amazon Exploration Series *Constantine Issighos*

Amazonian Tribes: A World of Difference 25

The Amazon Exploration Series   *Constantine Issighos*

Amazonian Tribes: A World of Difference

The Amazon Exploration Series   *Constantine Issighos*

Amazonian Tribes: A World of Difference   29

The Amazon Exploration Series *Constantine Issighos*

Amazonian Tribes: A World of Difference

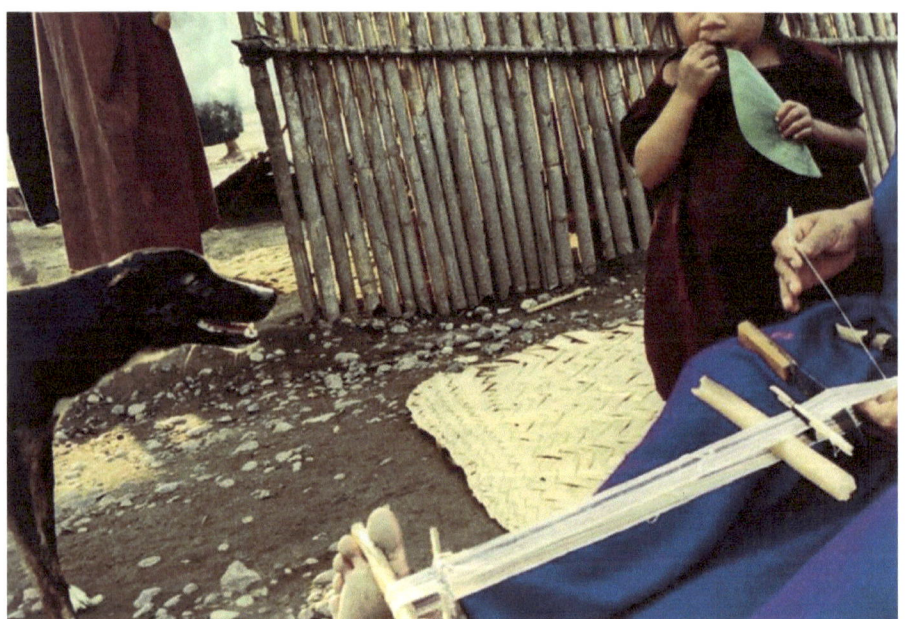

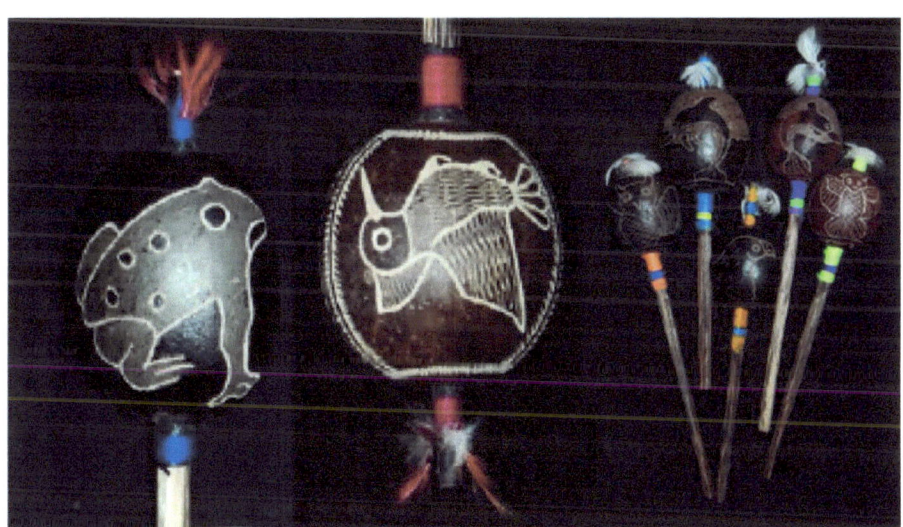

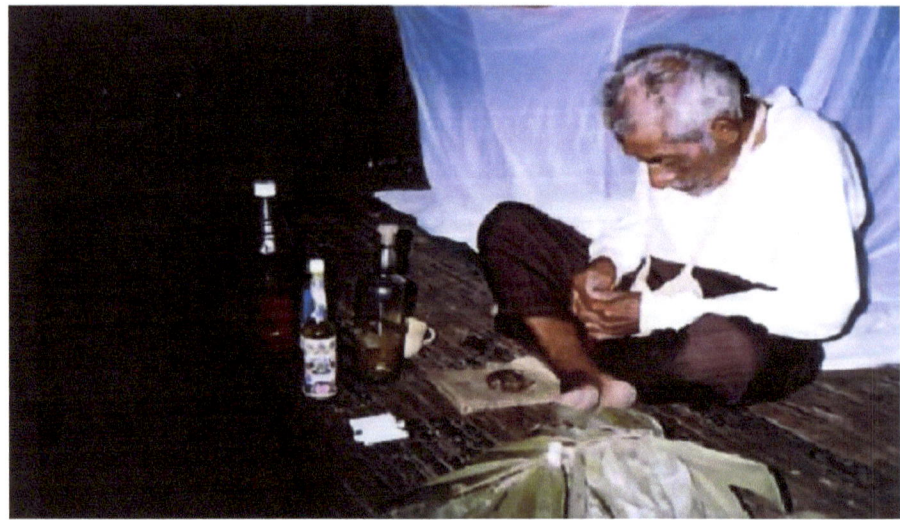

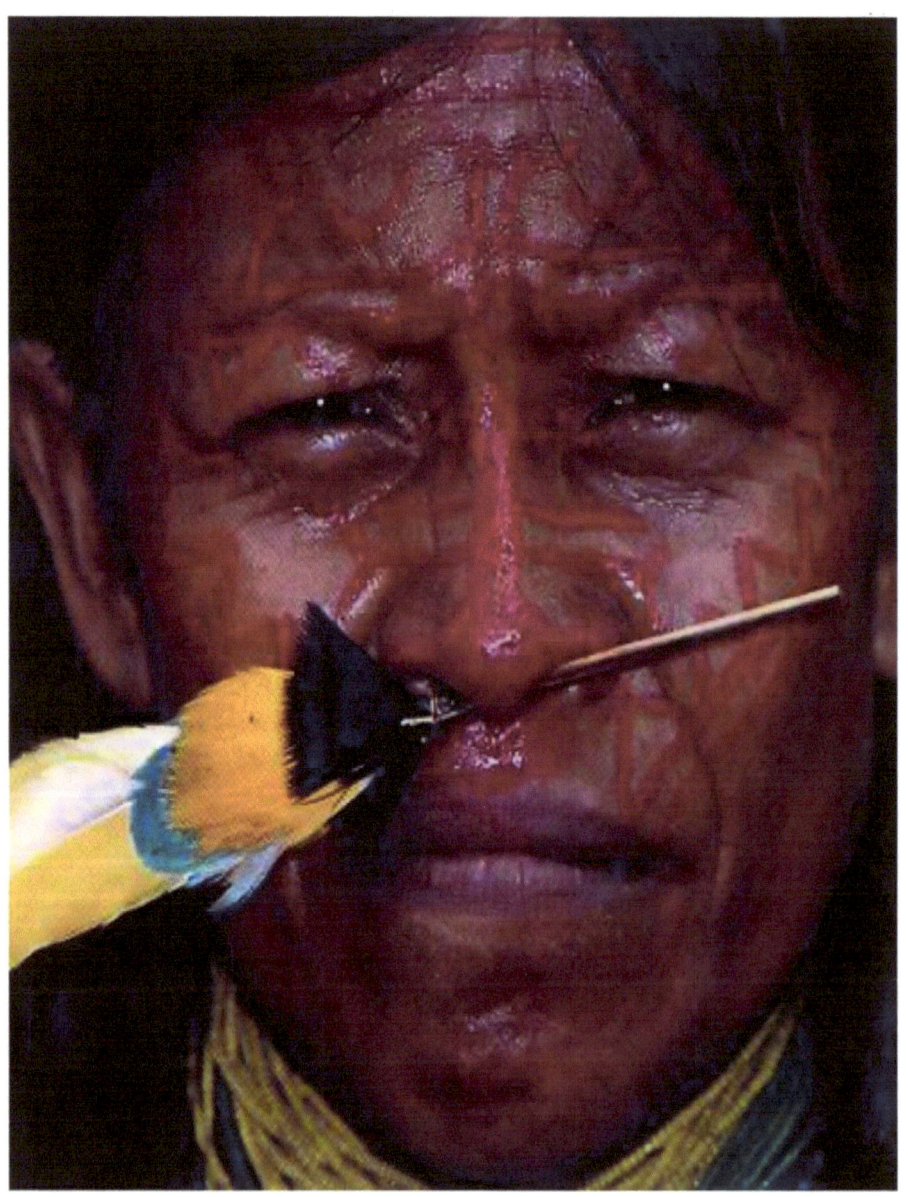

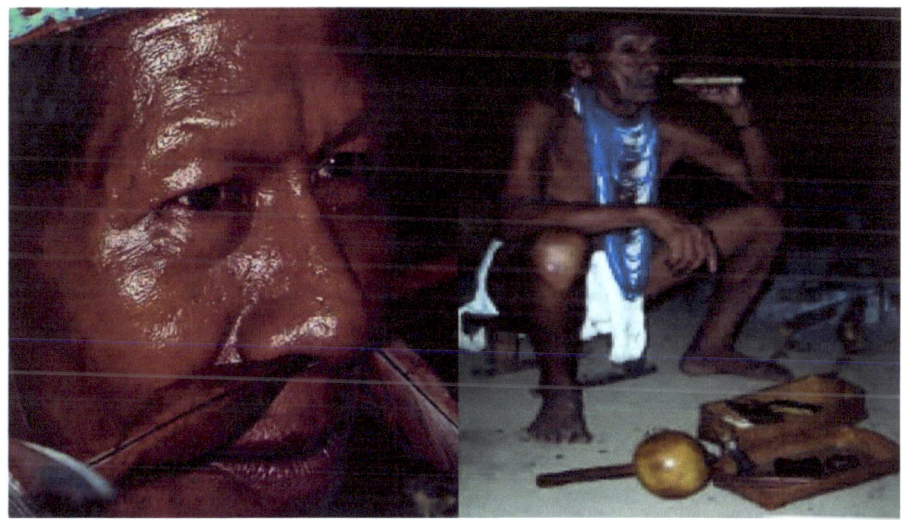

The Amazon Exploration Series *Constantine Issighos*

Amazonian Tribes: A World of Difference 45

The Amazon Exploration Series   *Constantine Issighos*

Amazonian Tribes: A World of Difference   *47*

The Amazon Exploration Series *Constantine Issighos*

Amazonian Tribes: A World of Difference 49

www.ingramcontent.com/pod-product-compliance
Lightning Source LLC
Chambersburg PA
CBHW041754040426
42446CB00001B/33